GLOBAL SUMMIT FOR CLIMATE CHANGE

Understanding COP28, its Global Importance the Fight Against Global Warming

John Wolf

Table of Contents

Introduction

The warmest September on record has been reported worldwide by the National Oceanic and Atmospheric Administration (NOAA), with September 2023 being the fourth consecutive record-warm month. There is a 99% chance that 2023 will wind up being the warmest year on record based on the maximum surface temperature recorded during the year. Four overarching topics will be addressed at the COP28 climate conference in the United Arab Emirates, which is slated to take place from November 30 to December 12: finance, inclusion, frontline communities, and technology and innovation. The information emphasizes how vital it is to address the root causes of climate change and mitigate its effects.

CHAPTER 1

What is Cop28 and why does it matter?

The 28th UN climate summit, or COP28, is scheduled to take place in Dubai, United Arab Emirates, from November 30 to December 12, 2023. There, leaders will deliberate on how to control global warming and get ready for its effects.

What is Cop28?

World governments have been meeting yearly for about thirty years now to discuss the climate emergency. As per the 1992 UN Framework Convention on Climate Change (UNFCCC), all nations are required to prevent severe climate change and develop fair global strategies for reducing greenhouse gas emissions.

What is COP?

The term "Conference of the Parties," or "COP," refers to a body that is established following the signing of an international treaty and is charged with making decisions on the treaty's implementation.

For every form of international accord, from combatting chemical weapons to preventing desertification, there is a COP. However, the name "COP" has evolved to refer to gatherings of a specific committee that was established following the United Nations Framework Convention on Climate Change (UNFCCC) signing.

Who is coming to COP28?

There have been over 200 governments invited.

Though both nations will be represented, it is unlikely that Chinese President Xi Jinping and US President Joe Biden will be present.

King Charles will also be there, as announced by Buckingham Palace, along with UK Prime Minister Rishi Sunak. On December 1st, he will give delegates an introductory speech.

Owing to sickness, Pope Francis has canceled his scheduled visit.

There will be participation from corporations, church organizations, think tanks, community groups, and environmental charities.

At COP27 in 2022, hundreds of delegates with ties to fossil fuels were present.

What are COP summits?

To stabilize greenhouse gas concentrations, a group of countries known as the Conference of the Parties (COP) ratified the UN Framework Convention on Climate Change (UNFCCC) in 1992. They've gotten together yearly ever since. In November 2022, nearly 100 chiefs of state and delegates from 200 nations convened for the most recent COP27. Funding for losses and damages was to be given to nations at risk from the effects of climate change. António Guterres, the UN Secretary-General, praised this as a major step in the direction of justice. A promise to keep increases in global temperatures to 1.5°C and a change from climate pledges to climate action were among the other commitments made.

Will there be an agreement on fossil fuels?

There will probably be disagreements on what to do with "unabated" fossil resources like coal, oil, and gas in the future. Mr. Jaber is in favor of "phasing down" their usage, but the EU and other organizations are anticipated to press for a complete "phase out". Restricting agreements to "unabated" fossil fuels, according to climate campaigners, would let some production to continue, as there are now more fossil fuels being produced or developed than could be used to keep warming to 1.5C.

CHAPTER 2

Will richer countries pay for climate change?

A "loss and damage" fund has been established by COP28 with the goal of compensating poorer nations that have been impacted by climate change for their substantial contributions. The fund, approved at COP27, is seen as a critical first step toward fostering mutual trust between wealthy and developing nations. Developed nations promised in 2009 to provide poor nations $100 billion annually to assist them in lowering their emissions and being ready for climate change. Despite not meeting the goal in 2020, early evidence indicates that it will probably be accomplished by 2022. The purpose of COP28 is to decide how to move forward with the $100 billion promise.

Will COP28 make any difference?

The term "greenwashing" refers to the practice of nations and corporations promoting their climate credentials without making the required adjustments, as charged at prior COPs. Beyond national boundaries, these summits do present the possibility of international accords. For instance, the 1.5C warming limit set at COP21 has sparked "near-universal climate action," which has lowered global warming levels, but current global action is not keeping up with what is required to meet the Paris targets.

When does it start?

A conference on climate action is being held in the United Arab Emirates beginning on November 30. On December 1st and 2, world leaders will gather for a summit, which will be followed by discussions on December 12th. Though past history indicates they may continue, the discussions are anticipated to end.

Why do we need a Cop – don't we already have the Paris agreement?

A conference on climate change is being held in the United Arab Emirates beginning on November 30. On December 1st and 2nd, world leaders will gather for the global climate action summit, which will be followed by discussions. Although December 12 is when the discussions are supposed to end, past performance indicates they can go on. Countries agreed to limit global warming to 1.5C and maintain temperature increases below 2C over pre-industrial levels under the terms of the Paris Agreement. They did, however, agree on non-binding national emissions reduction goals for greenhouse gases by 2030. It was decided that these goals, referred to as nationally determined contributions (NDCs), would not be sufficient to keep the global temperature within the Paris objectives. The accord included a "ratchet mechanism" that the French included, mandating that nations reconvene every five years with new promises. The five-year period concluded on December 31, 2020, and nations established new goals at Cop26 in November 2021.

Didn't all this get sorted out at Cop26?

Countries decided at COP26 to concentrate on the 1.5C objective set by the Paris Agreement since a 2C increase would result in disastrous climate effects. Since the agreement, research has demonstrated that a 2C rise would have permanent consequences. At Cop26, a number of nations revised their national Determinants of Climate Change (NDCs), and the nations that account for three-quarters of the world's greenhouse gas emissions established long-term goals to achieve net zero carbon by the middle of the century. But in order to keep global warming to 1.5C, emissions must be cut in half from 2010 levels and the globe must achieve net zero by 2050. During the Glasgow meeting, nations decided to speed up the ratchet mechanism by mandating yearly updates on NDCs and pushing for additional NDC submissions until they meet the required standards.

What has happened since?

Vladimir Putin's invasion of Ukraine in February 2022 sparked a worldwide crisis that resulted in the reshaping of alliances and partnerships. Prior to Putin's invasion, energy costs were already growing, but the conflict in Ukraine sent gas prices over the roof. Putin cut off supplies, threatened to withhold supplies, and interfered with the Nord Stream pipeline in order to utilize Europe's reliance on Russian gas as a weapon of war. Gas prices increased as a result, and fossil fuel businesses profited handsomely, setting records in the process. In order to combat this issue, the EU has launched a campaign for energy efficiency, imposed a windfall tax on the excess profits of fossil fuel firms, and promoted the use of renewable energy sources. A few EU nations have also started looking for fresh sources of fossil fuels, developing terminals for liquefied natural gas, and investigating potential gas fields. In 2021, the International Energy Agency issued a warning, stating that if global warming stays below 1.5C, no further fossil fuel production is possible.

CHAPTER 3

What happened at Cop27 last year?

A major occasion for developing nations demanding compensation for the "loss and damage" brought on by climatic issues was Cop27 in Egypt. Developed nations decided to set up a fund to give money to the most vulnerable and impoverished nations impacted by climate disasters. But this accord was only the beginning. Countries in the Cop28 must figure out how to make the fund a reality because loss and damage is still a divisive topic at Cops.

Isn't the UAE an oil-producing country?

With its enormous gas and oil reserves, the UAE has selected Sultan Al Jaber to lead Cop28. Protesters and several nations objected to Al Jaber's selection as the first businessman to hold the position of Cop president. Al Jaber, however, sees the position as a logical progression because there would be no solution to the global catastrophe without the fossil fuel industry. He is an ardent supporter of the global energy system's reform and co-founded Masdar, a renewable energy firm supported by the UAE government, in 2006.

The UK, which is hosting Cop26, has experienced a dramatic shift in perspective. Rishi Sunak removed Alok Sharma, the UK president of Cop26 under Prime Minister Boris Johnson, from the cabinet in the fall of last year. Although Sunak claims to be a "climate leader" with "world-beating" accomplishments, the majority of the carbon reductions he claims to have achieved occurred during earlier administrations. In addition, Sunak has publicly reversed course on net zero policy, delaying the phase-out of gasoline and diesel vehicles, which has further distanced the UK from fulfilling its legally-mandated goal of achieving net zero greenhouse gas emissions by 2050.

In addition to launching a significant round of new licenses and vowing to "max out" the North Sea, Sunak is also drafting new regulations that will mandate yearly license auctions. This year, he was absent from both the UN secretary general's climate summit and the UN general assembly. King Charles III, who was refused permission to attend and give a keynote address at Cop28 last year, will be permitted to attend.

Are we nearly there on 1.5C at least?

This year's record temperatures have risen to more than 1.5C above pre-industrial levels, more than they have in the previous 100,000 years. Global records were broken and ocean temperatures were characterized as "globemaking bananas." The El Niño weather system is having a major influence on the situation, even if average temperatures are still marginally below the 1.5C barrier.

What About The UK?

Because they anticipate a longer trend before declaring the limit passed, scientists do not consider one, two, or three years of temperatures above the 1.5C threshold to be a violation of the Paris Agreement. But more significant carbon reductions are required to keep the temperature at 1.5C.

Why is 1.5C so important?

According to the Intergovernmental Panel on Climate Change (IPCC), the earth will suffer considerable harm with a 1.5C temperature increase, with the harm from a 2C increase differing significantly. It is thought to be safer at the lower temperature. Even so, a 1.5C increase would still cause sea levels to rise, coral reefs to bleach, and more heatwaves, droughts, floods, and storms. The most recent IPCC assessments, which have been released after Cop26, have emphasized these cautions and come to the conclusion that, although it would take coordinated efforts, there is still a remote likelihood of remaining below the 1.5C barrier.

How far do we have to go?

The earth's temperature has risen by 1.1–1.2C since pre-industrial times, and greenhouse gas emissions are still rising. Although carbon dioxide emissions decreased during the Covid-19 lockdowns, economies rebounded. However, this decade, global emissions must fall by 7% yearly to sustain 1.5C.

CHAPTER 4
What about net zero?

By the middle of the century, all greenhouse gas emissions must be eliminated in order to prevent global warming to 1.5C. Any leftover emissions must be offset by expanding the world's carbon sinks, such as wetlands, peatlands, and forests. Long-term objectives, however, are insufficient since carbon dioxide remains in the atmosphere for almost a century after release and the climate reacts to accumulated emissions. Even if we reach net zero by 2050, we might irreversibly surpass the 1.5C barrier. The 2020s are referred to as the "crucial decade" for the climate by scientists because, with early peaking and quick reduction of emissions, we can keep cumulative emissions from increasing too high and have a chance of keeping below 1.5C.

Is Cop28 just about 1.5C?

In order to evaluate global progress in reducing greenhouse gas emissions, the Paris Agreement talks are centered upon the National Development Goals (NDCs). For poor nations, climate financing is essential since it offers funds from both public and private sources to assist in reducing emissions and mitigating the effects of extreme weather. The OECD's early data suggests that the aim of $100 billion annually by 2020 was likely fulfilled last year and will almost probably be met this year, despite its missed deadline. Many concerns, meanwhile, are still unresolved. One such issue is the distribution of climate funding, with the majority of the funds going to middle-income nations for emissions-reducing initiatives like solar or wind power.

Rich nations have committed to increasing climate funding for adaptation by double in Cop26, but developing nations still hope to make major headway in this area in Cop28. Increasing funding in the form of grants rather than loans has the potential to increase a nation's debt. The difficult problem of loss and damage—the most catastrophic effects of extreme weather that no amount of adaptation can lessen—is one area where climate financing shines. It can take years for developing nations to recover from such destruction, and during that time, their chances of improving their populations as well as their infrastructure and health and education systems may be permanently harmed.

Countries decided to establish a new fund for loss and damage at Cop27 last year, but disputes soon grabbed control. A few weeks ago, a solution was struck, with the fund being temporarily handled by the World Bank and distributed to the most vulnerable and impoverished nations. Developed nations have been sluggish to contribute fresh funds, and there is no consensus on how to replenish the funds. Most nations acknowledge that their governments alone will not be able to fill the fund; instead, new funding sources will be required. This may include fees on shipping and frequent fliers, sales of tightly controlled carbon credits, and windfall taxes on oil and gas revenues.

What about China?

China, the biggest emitter in the world, wants to cut carbon output per GDP unit by 65%, attain net zero emissions by 2060, and peak emissions by 2030. Following their November meeting in California, US and Chinese climate envoys John Kerry and Xie Zhenhua decided to include non-CO_2 gases in their National Decadal Progress Reports (NDCs). According to a recent study, China's rapid increase in renewable energy may be moving the nation closer to a tipping point, which may lead to a peak in world emissions as early as next year. That being said, this is still a big if.

This is the 28th Cop – why has all this taken so long?

The contemporary world has been mostly dependent on fossil fuels since the industrial revolution, ushering in a Promethean period where cheap, readily available energy is the foundation of wealth and technology. It will need major adjustments to the built environment, transportation, energy systems, behavior, and food to end this dependency. While developing nations want ongoing usage for economic progress, developed nations have been averse to the expenses. Politics has been impacted by disputes about historical accountability, burden-sharing, expenses, and science. But in much of the globe, green technology and renewable energy are now more affordable than fossil fuels, and the development of electric car technology has accelerated. Countries like the US, who pulled out of the Paris Agreement, hold the key to the destiny of our world.

1. The world is "woefully off-track" when it comes to achieving the 17 UN Sustainable Development Goals and the Paris Agreement, the UN Secretary-General has warned. Since most agreed-upon international climate objectives are incorporated inside these accords, a "global stocktake" to assess progress, pinpoint areas of failure, and redouble commitment to ensuring climate promises are translated into action will be place during COP28.

2. According to a research that was published in Earth System Science Data, greenhouse gas emissions are at an all-time high. Although the rate of emissions is decreasing, the 1.5°C objective set out in the Paris

Agreement is now in danger. This is a crucial decade since rates of global warming caused by humans are at an all-time high, and during the next ten years, 1.5°C global warming may be reached or surpassed. A major topic of debate at COP28 will be how to expedite the energy transition in a way that is both inclusive and sustainable. Topics of discussion will include how to quickly scale up renewable energy sources, as well as novel ideas like hydrogen fuels and carbon capture technology. In order to guarantee a just transition, delegates will also search for measures to guarantee that minority populations and developing countries benefit equally from it.

3. Global air pollution and water scarcity in underdeveloped nations are two major

health effects of climate change. A full day of the COP conference will be devoted to programs that safeguard lives and livelihoods, foster community resilience, and advance peace. There will be high-level talks on health, relief, peace, and recovery, with a focus on conflict-affected areas and the difficulties in mitigating and adapting to climate change. In order to combat the growing consequences of climate change, this is a crucial step.

4. In order to influence the conversation during COP28 Trade Day, the World Economic Forum is collaborating with the United Arab Emirates, UNCTAD, the World Trade Organization, and the International Chamber of Commerce. The forum's goal is to fairly finance climate action and adaptation, with a

focus on poor nations who bear a disproportionate amount of the burden of the climate catastrophe. Leaders from the government, business, and philanthropy sectors will come together at the conference to unveil many public-private philanthropic collaborations. In addition, the forum is collaborating with the COP28 Presidency to investigate possible ways to finance the net zero transition, with an emphasis on the economics of food, agriculture, and natural ecosystems. Ensuring that all stakeholders, especially those in developing nations, have access to reasonable financing for sustainable development is the aim.

5. The goal of COP28 is to get more leaders involved in transforming climate commitments into action. Mayors,

governors, corporations, and non-governmental organizations (NGOs) that are instrumental in putting climate policy into action at the local and regional levels will come together at the COP28 Local Climate Action Summit. António Guterres, the secretary-general of the United Nations, highlights the need of enlisting local governments and providing them with the resources and ability to expedite climate action. The role of city leaders in accelerating the energy transition, fixing climate finance, focusing on people, lives, and livelihoods, and making sure local voices are heard at the international climate table was highlighted by COP28 President-designate Dr. Sultan Ahmed Al Jaber. Global risk perception is dominated by climatic and environmental concerns, with the most important need in the coming ten years being to not worsen climate change.

CONCLUSION

In conclusion, the world is facing an unprecedented climate crisis, and it is imperative that we take immediate action to address the root causes of climate change and mitigate its effects. The COP28 climate conference in the United Arab Emirates is a crucial opportunity for world leaders to come together and make significant progress on this critical issue. The four overarching topics of finance, inclusion, frontline communities, and technology and innovation provide a comprehensive framework for addressing the climate crisis. I urge world leaders to seize this opportunity and make bold commitments to reduce greenhouse gas emissions, invest in renewable energy, and support vulnerable communities. Thank you for reading and for your commitment to protecting our planet.